self-driving

ALSO BY BETSY FAGIN

Names Disguised (Make Now Books)

All is not yet lost (Belladonna)

Fires Seen From Space (Winter Editions)

self-driving

by Betsy Fagin

Winner of the 2024 Autumn House Press Poetry Prize

PITTSBURGH, PA

self-driving

ISBN: 9781637681107
Published by Autumn House Press

Cover Art: *untitled* by Sara Shapouri, acrylic and ink
Book and Cover Design: Melissa Dias-Mandoly
Author Photo: Lisa Mackie

Library of Congress Cataloging-in-Publication Data:
Names: Fagin, Betsy author
Title: self-driving / by Betsy Fagin.
Description: Pittsburgh, PA : Autumn House Press, 2025.
Identifiers: LCCN 2025010916 (print) | LCCN 2025010917 (ebook) | ISBN 9781637681107 paperback acid-free paper | ISBN 9781637681152 epub
Subjects: LCGFT: Poetry
Classification: LCC PS3606.A2657 S45 2025 (print) | LCC PS3606.A2657 (ebook) | DDC 811/.6--dc23/eng/20250715
LC record available at https://lccn.loc.gov/2025010916
LC ebook record available at https://lccn.loc.gov/2025010917

Printed in the United States on acid-free paper that meets the international standards of permanent books intended for purchase by libraries.

Autumn House Press is a nonprofit corporation whose mission is the publication and promotion of poetry and other fine literature. The press gratefully acknowledges support from individual donors, public and private foundations, and government agencies. This book was supported, in part, by the Greater Pittsburgh Arts Council and the Pennsylvania Council on the Arts, a state agency funded by the Commonwealth of Pennsylvania.

for fellow travelers

CONTENTS

SHARING THE ROAD

Flex

That was pretty mean, even for police.
We drive beyond smoke-flashed rivers'
enchanted redness (*the water still burns*).
Soon was abrupt, got mouthy, curt like gas
pump business transacting with future's heights.
Descriptions of words never said in small towns
of Cokes where moonlight is imprisoned, but escapes
like desperadoes to the California new. Imperious
with countryside cushion backs. Myself bare-
chested, unshaven, we limousined like conscious
people through drowsy towns. A prayerful tell-all.
His preyed road eyes who's got next, who font
splendid facts, but muddy themselves in their haste.
Wine bottle on the railroad, sitting for a moment
between junction nightfall and now.
This day is like a car crash. Pour some out.
Tuesday as fuck. Keep testing me.

Jetstar

What closer and closer came, what was faint
then dark and suddenly, furiously barking dogs!
Suddenly skies! Tingling, we belong where earth
pinned us. Held in its heaviness. The dew breeze
air still somewhere around here. Brakes slammed
across the dawn. Crow began. Roosters awake.
Swamp and trees living among us, palpable.
The air never air. Not atmosphere of all our breaths
deep and shallow, mouths open in slack-jawed
indifference. Make me above the sky's open branches.
No arms outstretched can steel us. Our bed,
the whole town sleeping guardian, suspicious
America wrought God and policemen lovely, lonely.
In their image. Their turned away sadness and
reluctance. Sleep meant this road. The road we're on.

Ranchero

Antique fields joked with local ranchers.
Here the gas stopped. We slowly rolled along,
wheel over to see the raw world school us,
whispering in my ear like that new car smell.

Supply chain driven by fear this whole time.
Steered toward safety, away from imagined lack,
real loss. The lies I told myself, all dust now.
Front cool, congealed thought, amalgamated.

Turn inward not to hide, but to explore. Arms
skyward through the hydrosphere, ecstatic collapsing
of external order: roadhouse, white house, madhouse.
People favor clothing with holsters built right in.

Intrigue

Thin glass threaded
ladies stick shift
from abject cold
toward a waning sun.

Dark now, the lone road,
steady focus on what
they say about you
when backs are turned.

Starliner

A nation so silent this whole time
building another highway while
women learned from crystal memory
and direction dug up from within.
Mined silence. Frantic now.
Sorrowful stillness pierced nerves,
no flinching. Forgiving gaze
and tender child eyes like they
breathed through all aspects and still
got asked for proofs. For identification.
Innocent presence, being brown, being flesh.
Great crystal rock, ithmid, sold to better see.
Road shoulders in all colors. Hunched air
grew cooler as we climbed.

Mainline

Sick of weathering life's complexity,
forged into an impossible
to understand night. Mountain ranges
pull sympathies toward looking more
than broken after the relationship fell apart.
Bold love, a toast to life. Table feed.
Always cycle, weather or not.
Dreams already gone. Some
forever, always, only. As if flesh
can nourish an outer limit
grown dark again, delicious.

Terrain

beautiful mosaic
dream frenzy wandered

sorrowful streets alone
drenched in morning coffee

lake ancient ditch bottom
bad water like underfunded

public schools, little sewers
and open rubble alleys

not what I wanted for my kid
would weed selling over

crucifix field hospitals
our long-suffering afforded life

Century

enormous slow
squat low, I ran

and ran, cycled
then drove. I traffic.

Downtown's statement
is not an apology.

I siren through
all obstruction.

Dodge and weave,
urgently American.

A girl can dream
of flowing

through boulevard
drive, getting nowhere

and everywhere at once.
Race to healing

or insurrection,
not the tagged toes

of cold bodies now
corpses. I sigh-scream

in endless cycles just
to look another person

up close in the eye,
surrender helpless.

Liberty

Barefoot yelling at mechanical lights,
frantic in theaters and cafés, imposed upon
like my fake name on the side of disposable cups,
like some people's net worth. A sudden burst
of almost-speech, pulled right up to standing
to pay the baristas a bureaucrat's wage, low-level
living as the earth quakes the jungle city off-center,
employee name tags calling everyone dead inside.

Do we talk to each other, or only men get to talk?

Posting up dream houses, dream closets,
dream weddings, whole-assed color schemes,
recipes to make, celebrities to follow,
restaurants to eat at when there's restaurant eating
again: Best romantic places in Phoenix.
Best places with gluten-free food. Paid good
money for 3,890 followers to like every little thing.

Crossfire
(keep quiet, baby here)

loyalties wander idling
skyfall for lucky children,
their open mouths

and grasping hands
picked personally,
tenderly. Promising

I'll keep us safe.
Better me than you.
I can take it.

Firenza

(good water, good place to camp)

Get someone else to fix the backed-up
names and profile pics while I torch,
very come-hither, creeping around
like some charity's year-end appeal
serving bargain basement wine.

Rewilding Denver, made holy again
at least around the airport. Coyotes
Land Back through underground tunnels
from boreal forests, keeping to the water's
edge to recolonize their territories.

Infinitely thirst quenching, off with
our sweat, drenched in remembered joy.
We are passionate people, resurging tender,
with native plant minds and rain gardens
restoring us all together again.

Aurora

Each of the mountains had its own name.
A name that spoke seeking, cast off shrouds
and mooring, unmoved. Sky shaping shifts
into spectacular, taught me to think of all as us.

Mountains as trees used to be, as skies are
always. Precious miles of awe driven by wishes
and private concerns, very expensive fuel.
Sweat dies and is sweat reborn then non-sweat.

Is it hot in here or is it just me?

Elite

(great place for a handout)

Down a ravine, no foothold,
no way forward and just one
wish left from fairy magic.
A toast to the now, newly
examined flesh to fall
from the bone in exchange
for earning entire lives
called back from keeping
her hands to herself. Sitting
quietly while jumbo jets dump
manufactured ice where
the caps melted. Before we
parked they seen us,
keep watching my mouth.

Raider

Desert origin of immediate
dawn a ruse of onward rush,
expansion. Thinking only
of the road, paved America can
be the world, thinks it already is.

Gripping the wheel, crying
lonely exile and surrender
to hellcat tombstones of spirit
photography. Too old now
to cross new borders.

Those used-to-be American
outlaws, these are their routes.
Cut through with personal wars,
now here to claim us. Call us home.
As the natural world understands

a petulant child, the stuck-out face
knowing nothing of justice.
Kicking to uncover what's buried,
what screams, years unearthed.
Love is never a request for silence.

Good morning, my kings and queens

Sometimes I am powered
by the worlds of the dead
all energy focused, a weapon.

None of us gets out alive
however far or fast we travel.
I know the crying floor anchored,

led back on a leash, not ashamed
of my pain. I don't hide
what I am, how could I?

Contour

Ledge belly rubbing
is resourced, in choice
as car cropped patchwork
fields, enormous ravines
loaded up with immense.
Carried lost teeth for luck.

Dark and squat allowing
complexity a ring road near
the river. Elevated time became
an accelerated city, urgent:
An evening out would be great.
Something to believe in again.

Edge

Such soothing and pleasant sleep!
Down showered atmospheres became me.
Sweated or froze me, caressed me.
Touched that something deep
with, not weather, but my life itself,
my time. The nights of summer close in,
telling sweet lies, like the sky was black
night—to my face. My car as witness.

To become you overtakes skin caked.
We are our dead, clotting sweat
braced against every breeze, every wind
of change. Going in one direction, flat out.
Car roof steel up to me. To bright them
ankles, arms, chest, bullets written on us,
bitten already. Our imminent sleep,
as thousands already sleep. Noise only

an instant blackness in staying. Car sweat.
Suffering pools in the seat back, caught
on camera. The road blanketed in impossible
to traverse. Ground dirt to dust. Now black.
All rest. All light drowned here in oil.
Can't drink oil. Even if it's store-bought.
Broke down and dirty, barefoot. Like how
they see every young girl,

dark like that.

Eagle

Ghost town once rush,
a boom. They were only
here for the money.
Now we make do with smoke
lungs turned stone
splashing in the highway
bathhouse, so American.

It's still too early to say
I love you. Early I-love-you's
are a classic warning sign.
Look for other red flags,
trust your gut. See if you
recognize other threats
looming on the horizon.

Imperial

(authorities are alert)

rag king drinking
cups full of earth

darkened rivers
bless the night before

prairie justice
dims our stars

lands them together
in immensity, isolated

dreaming people
to a freedom road

no courts for kings
no cells for prisoners

Saturn

Waiting spectators
for a moment's second
sight before girls switched.
Old religions still practiced
today. Old magics not lost.
Repurposed symbols,

sigils, and signs. Freedom hex.
Girl again, courtesan, alley life
in rushed, all too brief afternoons.
Spectral dream fire fanned
like this longing could never change.
Opportunities posted up

even though he trash. Welter in
money, thrust wife to faithful
like rent was coming due. Cavort
with his friends, American, gladly.
Jumped back girl, dark, little. Othered.
Want her delirious with all this talk,

with her undress. Take her longing,
armed, I will better care her heart,
have it swallowed whole, shoes on,
ready to walk out. Already leaving
duress. I slept rough again last night.
Crazy year we had last week.

DEFENSIVE DRIVING

Camaro

(people do not give)

How many gods are left?
Let's count. Your money,
just paper,
can top the list.

Earth, wind, water, fire,
and heart with their powers
combined equal more
than half-dollars or pesos.

Mastodon, Pterodactyl,
Triceratops, saber-toothed
tiger, Tyrannosaurus rex all
come out of the volcano together

to unify the torn asunder
calling girls down into the pit
then back up: redeemed, holy.
Someone's daughter, girl-colored,

watching window men.
Mad written across her
every opening: sixteen-
year-old on a smoke break.

The room for just half
an hour. Bounce inside
like the loudspeakers, all
these dicks I didn't ask to see

luring the devil I know
into coves with air trumpets
of exorcism to destroy
enchantment. Walls of sound

showered downbeats
indifferent to sidewalk dirt,
broken glass, dead little rat.
Festive cops bystand, dancing

rainbow flags for the weekend.
Half my gay martyrs roll over
in their graves to give me all
the power-ups: lightning circle,

black robot, magnet that attracts
gems. We need everything and
already have everything we need.
Oops, wrong portal. My bad.

Windstar

I silence fires from lost time
and lowered consciousness,
continue to livestream paranoia

routine waking up not wanting
to get out of bed. It's warm here.
Nice. I feel comfortable. Savor

this warmth, the death of sleep.
Can life as wonderful for each
other (and ourselves) as possible?

Dreams void this waking world's
sleep. As though I myself was
a doorway, a threshold as any

woman is sunny streets, hot,
windows everywhere—open
to get inside. Sky pours gold

streams to nourish inner
riches hidden deep within
every glittering treasure box.

Summit
(nothing happens here)

Nothing to do but wait.
I have no proof only
now-flat champagne
and a breeze that blows
desert insistent.

So steady around here.
We need no walk slow,
no look cool. The sweetness
of the world overcoming
every desiccated heart,

every barren land all in black.
For show, for darkness was
the tree of life itself. Branches
root down gathering old lady words,
poems about flowers. Ripened fruit

in the poison garden
where all the plants can kill.
Housed is only waiting
to get back in the car.
To mother and brother,

to sibling or solitude. Make
monument lives of toxic gardens.
Contaminated or not, we build,
implode and presence to the top,
big up ancestors and future generations.

Dart
(poor people live here)

I loudspeaker over them,
record it back for future use.

If music wants them, why not
aim higher, court the sun?

Dance skyclad, boozing.
Girls found their true forms

in narrowed traffic, hard
merge crawling all over to obey

her every command.
Housecoat wearing, spent

like possible money in her
god-aspect still tender.

Looked eighteen. No sorrow
unknown. Arms all sons

as babies: little guns,
little cars already parked.

Expedition
(I went this way)

Just like other crying girls
with no names of their own—
paralyzingly shy, anxious
left alone on the tattered road.

Our suckled eyes from stare,
from comment thread, subject to
moneybags' self-importance.
Ostensibly history. The earth

is now cooperating with me,
sourced from mass graves.
Miles of walls rotted by wailing.
This world of ourselves is men

in the otherwise abandoned
city parks always watching,
leering, lurking. Driven by
reverie, I take the wheel.

Probe

Now I need sleep. You drive.

Even though it's time for change
that won't brink the country
to self-reflection. Steady,
country, we're coming for you.
An endless swamp of people
found tenderness subdued
into mad, red-streaked eyes
sweating tell-alls. Still,
someone loves them. Or
loved them once. Or could
maybe love them in the future.
Could this be the same sleeping
country and road this whole time?

Aveo

It was weird outside.
Sleep gave up completely
on feeling rested. Fiends
drive us ever onward.
Mexico City wants
Monterrey's excitements,

high enough to make the sun
behind the sun appear.
Forward-thinking and
long-term perspective burned
down because it could get more
from the insurance money.

Clouds written in enormous
sky's blue, past walls'
reach, its razor wire,
mirrored facade over smoke
manufacturing towns,
just like every wounded road.

Cliffside rapists' names
whitewashed into greatness
of precipice stone
and desert mesquite.
Hardly noticing our own.
The great road resumes.

Suburban

(crime happened here)

A country this alone?
Appropriating cowboy,
lonesome never: chaps,
hats, animals, the wide
open. What is alone?
How could that be?

Notice thrilling,
mysterious doorways,
side quests to other
dimensions' ever-
expanding fusion biverses
to liven up discretions.

Choice young moon
dark girls, strange from
huts with stick walls,
thatch tangled through
with bright ribboned
hopes for salvation.

Durango
(stay off main street)

Before us, Mexico. Having slept well,
I woke up to almost all the countries at once,
only a few left now would leave a body
half dead in Laramie like that.

Only these country wilds, a cactus and yucca
relationship, ghostly, between the land still
solid beneath our feet and the Gulf of Mexico
come over the levees. Enormous with continent,

up all hours. We never dreamed the extent
of our magic. Road life everything, Astrodome,
America wasted. Money used to go so far:
cents for cigarettes, beer in cold bottles, jukebox

guitar in the smoky lunchroom. Like the night
chairs old men settled into, cheek to cheek,
lights dull. All left feet in soft Mexico
as we angry mob embracing our weakness.

Mustang
(good road to follow)

All three Mexicos
are amazement muscled
from a stolen land—
I was here first,

my hand whole heart
a land of fists. Anything
that wasn't Mexican soil
now soon would be.

We don't know
from America, only Texas
that wakes Laredo sinister
from sleep. Through walls,

under fences. Transported
by magic from dry wells
to the river, hundreds
of dusty miles between us.

Aspire

Ease her out like an old Ford.
Kissing her to keep her from sleep,
an endless detour on some dirt road.
Creek thirsty near wilderness,

only our Texas heart keeps beating.
Night falls on the South while sidewalks
burn, capital in flames. Texans care
about Texas. Care contorted outlook

shot up and shipped. Salt them
lest they rise again. Abilene at first,
but slowly, undeniably Texas.
Walls now wandered among whites

where blues had been—blue ocean,
blue sky—sealed off, airtight.
Plot after plot, stories and graves,
all Amarillo from the way songs tell it.

Immense with abandoned gas stations,
tumbleweeds where full service once was.
Amarillo empty, still. Waste this mesquite
land, stop time. Worth driven through longing.

A highway moment of open expanse
demanding your keys, interpreting moods,
tracking biometrics and reporting back
to central. Nightmares of never again,

gone beyond the beyond to legendary.
A thoroughfare of freedom hewn
from wilderness, salvaged. The road
saves us from ourselves.

Starfire

(doctor lives here)

In the olden before
times, thousands
hitched the highways.
Our peak shadow still
beyond imagination.
Driving on doomed
and sinister, sent secret
corruptions roses, exotic
strange. Wait and see
if what hurts
is really broken.

Skyliner
(dry town)

Dissolved air became smoke as I retreated
to pleasant memories of Denver being only me.

I lived by myself, cooked for myself. No one
to answer to but myself. I knew my place

was everywhere. I knew my rights
were all the rights, my freedoms all the freedoms.

Now there is only walking everywhere, rock shades
of far-November's purple dusks. Brooklyn-like

to the mountains red as the sun made its way
across the heavens mapping out renewal and rest.

Solace creates force fields in the body that can
counteract surrounding escalations even as we grow

increasingly vulnerable. Lose everything,
everyone. Even this. Goodbye old car.

Fifth Avenue

(money for work here)

Machine marked time
while we New York break room—
Marxist postcards of peanuts
and pennies before a lavishly
set table—having it all.
Several of us stuck together,
to form our own party uproar:
dancing where no dance
floor, water like whiskey
and beer like wine.

Cruiser

(good place to sleep)

Draped in mournful
diamonds of try harder
and longing. Concentrate
this maybe could into shine
bright, dirty pleasures. Silks
off night once home. Came.

Cold. Increasingly alone.
Reduced to games of win
and lose on Thursday streets.
Our real lives whole rivers away.
Snowmelt headwaters, bubbling
up into tributaries from depths.

It was said that she could hear
beyond hearing, see with inner eyes.
Us all one self, no other. Do not doubt
that the wait is necessary.
This window of time is longing
for home during an extended absence.

Another North Star

Know love as it's running
through you not idling
for career wealth mastery.
Family rich with hopeless
abandon pulsing through her
westward expansion
from room to room
over the whole house
or apartment. Open road
ecstasies bursting
in overgrown plots
with only two exposures
ever rushing to ruin banks,
waving wrath percentage
yield like rivers that make
their own silt roads.

Escort

(cowards; will pay to get rid of you)

Sidewalks proudly
trampled mornings hosed down
after being out all night.

Living dream snapshots
of troubled saints, our street
became livable once queer

artists blessed the front line.
Superhighway dusk red
spending from an owed wallet,

mortgaged, bank-backed house.
Catch me vanishing, dashcam car.
Check the bushes and behind the dumpster.

No more playing.
American hands grabbed
the wheel with only seconds left.

DRIVING EMERGENCIES

Scorpio

Water buried man-made paths sparking
thousands of chariots with jalopy wings.
Our gleaming eyes, our purpose plain
our faces, plains, pursuing speed
as enormous cloud approaches
and descends upon every road.
This job has whole lives to pay off.
I get the movie rights from when he lost
his temper and before she shaved her head
because life. Enough to make me signify.
Release talking points to the news networks
poking holes in your testament and bible whole.
Prison me in my pawnshop suit. Politicize my death.

Galaxie

Grapevine news ready to suck
the life out of us, gay dreams pre-plotted,
seeded according to algorithms.

Plumeria, kids playing in little yards.
We reclined to rest in comfortable
chairs, feeling we'd found our high noon.

When my heartfelt dreams get crushed
I just make new ones,
therefore my heart is invincible.

insert miracle here

Executive

(Have you ever stood on a factory floor?)

I only sense sleeping through valerian,
ashwagandha and CBD, leading me east
of myth, dark weird of west. Hear bedtime
stories of gallant cowboys, ever-singing
nightmare songs of unconditional love
in Istanbul and Sydney. They mean
unconditional fucking. Road end reached.
Hipsters start up rumor factories and content
mills for work. Jobs outsourced overseas
for cheaper non-union labor. Movie people
assemble while we're still mourning.
That was no accident.
We bus out like locusts, ragged and lost,
scream all summer, aching for what
we already are. Credit her, supporting life.
Spent her all-night shifts for these ditties.
Nourish her essential labor, infrastructure
like trees. She road cars watched, porch sat.
Every night feels hot, warm enough to hammock.

Encore

Would outfit the Roxy in roses,
visit New York, the big city, wishing
all summer as her grandmothers had.
Dreaming of what starlets they could be
if only discovered. What idea didn't she,
to be a star. Her take wanted life of you.
To what crying was. Having not blood her,
generations and generations back
that sunken emptiness gazing out
with eyes so dark even at her sex friends.
Was that fun for you?
She said she was glad you not heart her
because heart gladdened means just this:
I love you right now. Shrouded
in perpetual depression. Why settle
when she breasts beautiful, hips wide,
prestige and displayed that—low-cut,
high-hemmed—her gorgeous, animated
conversation gets the job done. Narrow
state roads roared on asleep, exhausted
into rural where log cabins feel private.
Who will be a star? Us all?

Tempo
(money here)

Cars in the truck lane
another bridge
burning in us up ahead.

Shrine of living—
no more celebrity
dead. No more

copycat, publicity
obsessed, stopping
mid-spree to check status.

Reconstituting civil
we embrace broken
vast, build anew

redistributing.
Resourced as foretold
in the stars.

Trailblazer

(get out of town quick)

Cadillac this
like drinking
muddy water (or oil).
Never in life my old
cuts going so deep.
Eventually the road
leads cars to wholeness.
South America maybe,
Panama and Mexico
down that road. Could we
dreamboat? Flotilla?
Gradually waters will
rise alongside the road.
A hold this tight,
this loving could car
magnificent and roar
as dreaming towns
startle themselves
back to sleep
in the moonlight.
I know we can
make good time.

Eldorado
(get bread here)

Boy sharp swords
at desert tourists to sell
bumper stickers for their sedans.
Profits sustain them through
this bad luck afternoon.

No car for me, I am open
to this unwinding. Could
all eyes closed so open?
Continent unfurling me.
Beneath some road,

bottomless deeps.
Rushing waves sunk
Atlantis, mourning
this crash, collapsing
our horrors.

Omega
(church people)

Old accidents arrive tonight
dancing across memory screens
of prior relaxation, recalled accords and
pawned watches recovered near the railroad.

Take this old man's story from him. He just
stares into middle distance now, hands shaking.
What he thought was his wife returning home
was just sounds from the street. She's been dead

how many years? Chain watch and vest, tweed
suit, jalopy out front. Suppertime in the afternoon—
crackers, maybe a few peanuts. Grayed memory
of love was lover to him now nightfall suffers.

Today's tortures: chairs sprawled, plastic covered
couch. Nobody to chaperone, ever-watching
incalculable boredoms forced to die alone
prematurely hidden from all light.

Valiant
(bad thing happened here)

Roared orders, lights
pulled up beside us.
Our chances look terrible.

Worn wild and dark,
complaining as gods
birthed in hidden light.

Accelerated after the first
warning shot telling me
it wasn't about race.

We road on regardless.
Magnificent, unprotected.
A harvest moon shines

on hair in the blood.
Wood fire days of waiting,
just jeans and fifteen.

Town & Country

See trouble much? Ever so, US
of A, the only gun road met all time
except without anything to eat, no extra
cents or ticket money, just time to kill.

Trouble sees the game, following
all the races. Looking past my lying
as confession, concluding my speech
about this beautiful glass life—full

or empty—already broken. Threat
comparison corny after investigation.
Sheriffs at home in delinquent county,
their license to arrest and operate

out-of-state needs inspection.
Lights and brakes to back in time,
to great nights, car stealing whole
days expressly for this trip

to age-falsifying Los Angeles.
A working road, right up until the end.
A woman could reach the coast in shades,
bejeweled, foil wrapped. Huddled

under staircases in our own filth,
we wanted to keep human. Made schedules
for ourselves, set easily attainable goals,
planned future destinations.

Taurus

(go around this town)

Thanks for several wasted nights.
This will all be over when we're arm in arm
in Laramie streets, stumbling past the riots,
covered in blood except where washed clean
by tears. The fence stayed stolen, resold on eBay.

Wretched refuse, very Cadillac.
Wanted voraciously, ate with both hands.
Podcasts enumerate perpetual distractions.

Monster truck those little spaces wide
in women. Ate abundantly at a well-built table,
cream risen to the top forever. Dairy industry
nostalgia dressed up quaint, in gingham,
like good times, good for you, nutritious.

New Yorker
("New blood, new rules.")

To hell with lit lamps
my fueled fire the long way
around walls decorated with
girls' rape whistles (souvenirs).

Darkness is campaigning:
no moon, no stars. Only
headlights across grief
mournful pastures. Winter

dramatizing incarceration
for entertainment. Plant that
seed in the mind: prison as fun.
I could have been your cellmate.

Voyager

Pretty in the face. Party friends. Street nights buried
struggle along dark roads. Our pilgrimage on foot.
Flowing beyond form and sound into the summer
road hot, standing attentive at the newly reinforced
border with which I am one. At home with myself.

Divorced, married, baby awful again. Nothing
logical in worry on the way out West. Always
know the road before attempting such a long journey:
unfamiliar with the driver's seat exerting will,
direction, shifting gears, invisible even to satellites.

I'll make a new map.

Escalade

(go this way)

Stolen bed, drunk bedroom
staggered in late in a dust battered
car. Mime face screaming something
about overcrowding and a juiced up
convertible, star-eating, infinitely
driving home. Found the driveway
writhing in agony. Terrified became reason.
So constant, pervasive. Everything terror
then. Sick for lost souls won't keep your car
from getting stolen. Told you not to park
at the crossroads. Your soul, for this?

Deluxe
(wet town / alcohol here)

A drunken frenzy barking
at the drum line, somebody's gay
cousin, triumphant. Foolish with money,

whiskey, and friends, the most oil-rich
countries in the world too drunk
to fuck. Danced all night then couched.

Wallpaper sad like shot-out tires
curse the calm. Everybody needs
someone and you have you, paranoid.

Background checking stay-at-home moms.
Their ugly words like street dogs' pack-dreams.
Frightened at trouble brewing.

Someone's looking good! Psst . . . it's you ♥

Alero
(hold your tongue)

Bashful was woman to her own touch,
sweat soft, sea-like where mountains
part from propriety. Semi-respectable
neighborhoods sprout up street lives,
their little dogs too—dressed in sports
uniforms, sweater-vests as seasonally

appropriate. Humans cry at night:
lost sleep pretending fields of perfumed
summer breeze, grateful children,
beautiful like their Pinterest pages.
Laughter from the crossroads, winter
driving solitudes. These are my family.

I'm never sorry, but I was wrong.

Achieva

Never in the passing lane,
stuck at the wheel crawling
night deserts. Car driving
autonomously. Diagnosing itself,

submitting reports, telling
on its passengers. Awake,
angel child, desert hysteria
no longer suppressed,

like they do girls. To asylum
must drive. To mutiny.
Relief to anyone needing
a lift, bearing witness

as even the best drivers collapse.
We are the traffic. Independent,
the car stopped suddenly. So,
are we there yet?

Enclave

How like you, facts
not feelings. A moment
of horror gasps then subsides.
People bond, connected
in tragedies, eyes face
roaring head-on. Hurled
into this moment, surely
the last. The show, over.
Yet the road runs on.
Clinging to our lives,
our loves are a noon
desert crossing, dosing
a panic-stricken dawn.
Keep promises vague,
and hold up half the sky.
All motives money
suspicious and sullen,
businesslike. Hotel room
too, bought and paid for.

Toronado

(easy marks)

The world messages you
just to play its favorite song.
Just to hear your breathing.

Bombed every holy city.
Every one. Seeming we and us,
we mourn—not marked safe, await

the next tragedy. Safe doesn't even
apply to me. Streets weary, worn
to ruins of chain stores, strip malls

to bandstand and mic grab excited
choruses. Thoughtful with the slow songs,
purple suit tattered. Echoing cries

for dueling at dawn. We all understand
the madness has him, no release.
Back-to-back lifetimes entranced,

cashed out on thoughts and prayers
across every platform, murderous lies
about forever. I believe in just this, fleeting.

Calais
(stay quiet)

Hands thoroughly
washed. Thought recoiled
from its defended position,
we are arrived. Never mind

home, stay here—
sexuality spilled all over
the carpet. Disciples now,
to our own self-mastery.

Clues left to help with pain.
Fortune cards lay out our plot.
Your mouth a canyon
of other dimensions, red

lights' consequence. Be careful
of who wants to save your
bitter silence. That removable
headrest could save your life.

Freestyle
(fake illness here)

Sidewalk cafés along the walk of suffering.
Torment: Paris, Rome. Let's New York.
Undone through numb America. Feverish,
motherless, battered, infected with idiocy,
bedeviled. Bloodshot eyes, wild hair, torn.
Horrible together, at the heart level.

Madness joins womanliness and loneliness
for a threesome. Suddenly, cream and sugar.
Fully actualized. Over ice. Floor moments
on my knees. Myself, all the selves, locked
away feeble, yelling through parlors. A sobbing
scene smiles for the cameras, just say yes. Say *yes*.

Trailhawk

(help if you are hurt)

You would save love to protect
inhabited visions such that
they feel so very real.
So yes and yes again
and yes until a brand-new mind
rearranged me. Conjured everything
including this Divisadero night
with those buses, nonstop.
We've been driven too far along
the wrong road, staring through the night.
Dry eyes, edges blur, the sides of the road
disappearing, as though all other cars are gone,
but they can't be. Are we scenic, washing lines
along the Hudson? Rivers running both ways,
immensely open to possibility, to changing
direction? Soothe the beast I am, belonging
to the river more than the highway.
Any country could be the land of our birth,
of powdered bones, blood spilled, sometimes
becoming courageous. Presente.

We will be plated in gold. Covered in crystals,
celebrate breaking open, wounds may never heal.

Equinox

Bled of sleep, broken down
the middle of the sidewalk.
What is it? Leaned against
a pillar for balance, you tell

me her many selves were
whole once, one road raged
through them all. She isn't
many, just one. Fractured

forever in traffic ecstasies,
new facets, facades where
shadowed wounds require
glamour to hide vulnerability.

I still feel you. We'll go
on foot, lighting up the town.
Different times soon come.
I swear it.

Meteor
(I ate)

As honey is sweet to me,
I know an off-ramp when I see one.
The fabled city at last: clouds pimped out,

shrouded what was haunted in us,
weather-beaten. Where covered wagons
rotted, people first became interested in heaven.

They rode on and so do we.
Pointing to the desert or salt-flat equivalent
of shattered bones, spent fires of mourning

and celebration gold sky. Starry night
polluted now with space-time, with all I do
is win. Late now, this joy. Too late maybe.

I performed myself as a life, heartbroken
illuminated flesh with the brights going through
childhood streets that knew me. America ecstatic,

detached women from our ancient rages
and rose arbors. Guardians of the veiled and love
locked. Woman guardian of the threshold,

protecting abandoned ambitions, muscles aching,
unfamiliar with the driver's seat,
exerting will, direction, concentrated force,

focus to lilac. Earth sad. Nobody wanders
anymore. Nobody. Lonesome America,
thinking myself saved, never leaving home.

NOTES

"Good morning, my kings and queens": This is a greeting Sandra Bland used in her *Sandy Speaks* videos before she was found dead, hanging in a jail cell three days after being taken into custody for a traffic violation in Texas in 2015.

"Executive": Conway Twitty, in his song "Don't Call Him a Cowboy," cautions "Don't call him a cowboy until you've seen him ride."

"New Yorker": For a time during the writing of these poems, there were posters in the New York City subway system advertising the fourth season of the television series *Orange Is the New Black*. "New blood, New rules" was the season's tagline. It found its way into this poem.

ACKNOWLEDGMENTS

Some of these poems were initially published in earlier forms. Many thanks to the publishers and editors of the following publications: *Beloit Poetry Journal*; *The Brooklyn Rail*; *Luigi Ten Co*; *No, Dear*; *Obsidian*; and *Superpresent*.

Gratitude to Kazim Ali for selecting this collection for publication, that it may be seen and shared. Thanks to Christine Stroud and everyone at Autumn House for their deep attention and great care with this work.

Special thanks to Sara Shapouri for creating the cover image that expressed precisely what I was trying to say. *Villmools merci* to Matvei Yankelevich for reacquainting me with the beauty and possibilities of language.

This work was written across many years. I appreciate the material support I've received from the Lower Manhattan Cultural Council, the New York Foundation for the Arts, and the Provincetown Community Compact.

I'm forever grateful to countless teachers and mentors who've guided me back to my own authority—deep bows to Thanissara and Kittisaro and all those whose generosity and kindness has helped me surrender to groundlessness with more confidence and ease.

Heartfelt thanks to my parents for their open minds and willingness to engage life with wonder and enthusiasm. Deepest love and gratitude to Lisa Mackie for sharing this journey with me. To my beloved Soil—Arti, Noah, Melina, emiko, Kareem—words fall silent, *you already know.* Thank you all for supporting me, bearing witness, resting deeply, and co-creating this new world.

NEW AND FORTHCOMING FROM AUTUMN HOUSE PRESS

Bigger: Essays by Ren Cedar Fuller, winner of the 2024 Nonfiction Prize, selected by Clifford Thompson

Interlocutor Goddess by Jasmine Reid, winner of the 2024 CAAPP Book Prize, selected by Aracelis Girmay

The Great Grown-Up Game of Make-Believe by Lauren D. Woods, winner of the 2024 Fiction Prize, selected by Kristen Arnett

Self Portrait as the "i" in Florida by P. Scott Cunningham, winner of the 2025 Donald Justice Poetry Prize, selected by Major Jackson

Les Portes by Meredith Nnoka, winner of the 2025 CAAPP Book Prize, selected by Cameron Awkward-Rich

Magdalena Is Brighter Than You Think by Grace Spulak, winner of the 2025 Rising Writer Prize, selected by K-Ming Chang

For our full catalog please visit: http://www.autumnhouse.org

WINNERS OF THE AUTUMN HOUSE PRESS POETRY PRIZE

Book of Kin by Darius Atefat-Peckham, selected by January Gill O'Neil

Taking to Water by Jennifer Conlon, selected by Carl Phillips

Seed Celestial by Sara R. Burnett, selected by Eileen Myles

speculation, n. by Shayla Lawz, selected by Ilya Kaminsky

under the aegis of a winged mind by makalani bandele, selected by Cornelius Eady

Cage of Lit Glass by Charles Kell, selected by Kimiko Hahn

Darling Nova by Melissa Cundieff, selected by Alberto Ríos

Apocalypse Mix by Jane Satterfield, selected by David St. John

St. Francis and the Flies by Brian Swann, selected by Dorianne Laux

Practicing the Truth by Ellery Akers, selected by Alicia Ostriker

The Moons of August by Danusha Lameris, selected by Naomi Shihab Nye

A Raft of Grief by Chelsea Rathburn, selected by Stephen Dunn

Natural Causes by Brian Brodeur, selected by Denise Duhamel

To Make It Right by Corrinne Clegg Hales, selected by Claudia Emerson

Gift that Arrives Broken by Jacqueline Berger, selected by Alicia Ostriker

heory of Everything by Mary Crockett Hill, selected Naomi Shihab Nye

The Dark Opens by Miriam Levine, selected by Mark Doty

No Sweeter Fat by Nancy Pagh, selected by Tim Seibles

lucky wreck by Ada Limón, selected by Jean Valentine

Naked Morning by Ruth L. Schwartz selected by Alicia Ostriker

Calf Kicks by Deborah Slicer, selected by Naomi Shihab Nye